The Ladybug...
Who Found Courage

By **Paige Benedetto**

Illustrated by **William Kirkpatrick**

This book is dedicated to our moms,

who taught us to be brave.

There once was a little ladybug named Red. Red was just a tiny bit different from other ladybugs.

She had an odd number of dots on her back. She had five dots, while every other ladybug had six.

Red knew she was different. There were times

when she felt alone.

Red's mom told her every night before she went to bed, that it was okay to be different, because being different made you special. Mother Nature made everyone unique, and if everyone were the same, life would be boring. Red always trusted her mom.

Soon the day came for Red to go to Springy-Fields Elementary School. She was afraid to leave her mom, but she was excited for the new adventure.

Red got on the caterpillar, waved goodbye to

her mom, and away she went.

When Red got to school, she met her teacher and her classmates. Most of them seemed nice and friendly.

However, there was one bumblebee that seemed to be a troublemaker. His name was Zap.

That night Red told her mom about all the exciting things that happened in school. Red's mom was so thrilled that her baby had fun while learning.

The next day in school Zap bullied Red. He
didn't like the fact that Red only had five dots.
Five dots meant she was different, and Zap
thought being different was bad.

When Red got home she sobbed to her mom while telling her about school. Zap scared Red, and she never wanted to go back to school again.

Every single day, for a whole month, Zap bullied Red. Little Red became very shy and frightened by Zap. Red's mom told Red that she should no longer let Zap squish her like a bug and to stand up for herself.

Red's mom then told a story of a time when she was bullied in school. Red's mom was born a darker shade of red.

All of the other ladybugs in her class were lighter and would call her names every day.

However, one-day Red's mom found something from within. She was sick of the other ladybugs making her feel bad about herself. So, she stood tall and told them to mind their own beeswax, because she was beautiful and she loved herself the way she was.

Red was fascinated by her mom's story. Red looked up to her mom even more now, because her mom did something very brave and Red was proud.

The next day came, and like clockwork, Zap

bullied Red. He told her she was a disgrace to

Springy-Fields Elementary School. However,

this time Red felt a fire within her heart. The

fire was courage.

Red stood up to Zap! She told him to go sting himself and to leave her alone. Red said that she loved her five dots and would not change anything about herself. Zap was shocked. He tried to say other mean things to Red, but his mean words could not hurt her feelings anymore.

Red was then thrown into the air by all the bugs

in her class, for standing up to Zap.

That night Red went home and told her mom what she had done. Red's mom gave her a hug and kiss, and told Red that she had the fire within her this whole time, it just took a little while for it to come out.

The next day in school, Zap tried to bully the other bugs in the class, but could not. They followed Red's example and stood up for themselves too. They were also proud to be different.

All of this happened, because Red found the fire within herself. She accepted that she was a little different from every other bug, and now she wouldn't have it any other way. Red loved being unique, because it made her special!

21078354R10018

Made in the USA
Middletown, DE
18 June 2015